Corvettes

By Kal Gronvall

Reading Consultants:
Gary Kelly and Pat Kelly
National Council of Corvette Clubs

CAPSTONE PRESS

MANKATO, MINNESOTA

C A P S T O N E   P R E S S
818 North Willow Street • Mankato, MN 56001

Printed in the United States of America.

Library of Congress Cataloging-in-Publication Data
Gronvall, Kal.
    Corvettes/by Kal Gronvall
    p. cm. -- (High performance)
    Includes bibliographical references and index.
    Summary: Gives an overview of the history of the Corvette sports car, covering some notable models and key people.
    ISBN 1-56065-391-4
    1. Corvette automobile--Juvenile literature. [1. Corvette automobile--History.] I. Title. II. Series: High performance (Mankato, Minn.)
TL215.C6G76 1996
629.222'2--dc20

                                                    96-27764
                                                      CIP
                                                       AC

Photo credits
Archive, 4. Behring Automobile Museum, 10. Carolyn Fitzpatrick, 14, 22-31, 37. FPG/John Crall, 33; Dean Siracusa, 34. National Corvette Museum, cover, 8. Unicorn/Dennis Thompson, 6, 42; Arni Katz, 11, 17; Fred D. Jordan, 16; Mike Morris, 18; Ronald E. Partis, 20; Paul Murphy, 38.
Visuals Unlimited/Mark E. Gibson, 12; Jeff Greenberg, 41.

Table of Contents

Words in **boldface** type in the text are defined
in the Glossary in the back of this book.

Chapter 1
The Corvette

The Corvette is one of North America's greatest sports cars. The Chevrolet division of General Motors makes the Corvette. Corvettes have **fiberglass** bodies. Fiberglass never rusts.

The Corvette was first made in 1953. Chevy has given it many different looks since then. Chevy has also made it one of the fastest cars in the world.

Collectors buy Corvettes because they increase in value as they get older. Corvettes made from 1953 to 1972 are worth the most money. Corvettes made from 1973 to 1982 are increasing in value, too.

The first Corvette was made in 1953.

Chapter 2

Birth of the Corvette

A man named Harley Earl designed a Corvette prototype in 1951. A prototype is a single car made as an experiment. Prototypes are developed into production cars. Production cars are the cars that are sold to the public.

Earl called the prototype Project Opel. Later, Earl called it the Corvette. He named it after a type of warship called the corvette. The corvette warship chased submarines during World War II (1939-1945).

The Chevrolet Corvette was first shown at the 1953 Motorama car show in New York

Corvettes made in 1953 are valuable to collectors.

Blue Flame 53

The National Corvette Museum

City. The Corvette's code name was the EX-122. People loved the EX-122.

A Fiberglass Car

A man named Ed Cole was Chevy's chief engineer. He wanted to build the Corvette with fiberglass. Fiberglass was developed for use in World War II. It was lightweight. It did not rust.

Chevy wanted to put a **V-8** engine in the Corvette. But they did not have one ready yet. They used an engine called the Blue Flame. The Blue Flame was a six-**cylinder** engine. It had 150 **horsepower**.

The Corvette was not very fast. Its top speed was only 108 miles (173 kilometers) per hour.

The First Corvette

The first Corvette rolled off the assembly line on June 30, 1953. Only 300 Corvettes were built that year. Buyers could not choose their cars' color. All 316 Corvettes were polo white with a sportsman-red interior.

The first Corvettes had an engine called the Blue Flame.

The 1953 models were made in Flint, Michigan. They were only sold to certain people. The general public did not have a chance to buy one.

The Corvette was a breakthrough in styling. But it needed more power. The Blue Flame engine was too small. The Corvette was too slow to be a real sports car.

The 1953 models are **collectibles**. They are valuable because there are not very many of

Only 200 1953 Corvettes exist today.

Chevy built 3,640 Corvettes in 1954.

them. Only 200 of the 1953 Corvettes still exist.

Poor Sales

The Corvette assembly plant moved to St. Louis, Missouri, in 1954. Chevy built 3,640 Corvettes that year. This time, buyers could choose from four colors: polo white, pennant blue, sportsman red, and black.

11

Chevy did not sell many of the 1954 Corvettes, though. People did not like the automatic transmission. A car with an automatic transmission shifts gears on its own. People thought a real sports car should have a manual transmission, with a **stick shift**.

People also complained about the Corvette's leaky convertible tops. Because sales of the 1954 Corvettes were so poor, Chevy built only 700 Corvettes in 1955. The 1955 model is a collectible, too.

The Corvette Versus the Thunderbird

The 1955 Corvettes had Chevy's first V-8 engines. Their top speed increased to 118 miles (189 kilometers) per hour. But even with the V-8 engine, Corvettes did not sell well. They could not beat their competition.

The Ford Motor Company had introduced the Thunderbird that same year. The Thunderbird was made of steel rather than fiberglass. Ford had already proved that it

Sales of the 1954 Corvettes were poor.

made a good V-8 engine. The public liked the Thunderbird better than the Corvette.

Zora Arkus-Duntov

Zora Arkus-Duntov was a Russian-born race car driver. He was also an engineer at General Motors. His job was to turn the Corvette into a race car. He is known as the father of the Corvette.

Arkus-Duntov beefed up the V-8 engine to 240 horsepower. The Corvette got faster. Sales were much better in 1956. But the Thunderbird was still more popular.

Fuel Injection

The 1957 Corvette offered a fuel-injected engine as an option. The fuel injection system replaced the engine's **carburetor**. The fuel injection system worked better than a carburetor.

The **fuel-injected** Corvette was called the Fuelie. It was the first fuel-injected car built in North America. Collectors value Fuelies for that reason.

Zora Arkus-Duntov is known as the father of the Corvette.

The Fuelie had a 283-cubic-inch (4,641-cubic-centimeter) V-8 engine. The engine produced 283 horsepower. It had a top speed of 140 miles (224 kilometers) per hour.

The Corvette Pulls Ahead

In 1958, Ford added a back seat to the Thunderbird. Sports car lovers no longer considered it a real sports car. The Corvette took over the sports car market. Arkus-Duntov's racing Corvettes got faster every year. By the late 1950s, they were winning almost every race they entered.

The 1957 Corvette was offered with a fuel-injected engine.

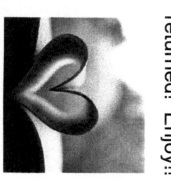

The 1962 Corvette was the last of the first generation.

In 1962, Chevy put a 327-cubic-inch (5,363-cubic-centimeter) engine in the Corvette. This engine had 360 horsepower. Even though it was faster, it still looked like the earliest Corvettes.

With cars, generations change when body styles change. The 1962 model was the last of the first-generation Corvettes. The next year, a new body style signaled a new generation.

Chapter 3

Change in the 1960s and 1970s

Chevy changed the Corvette's body style in 1963. The new model was called the Sting Ray. It was an immediate success. It had either a **fastback** or a convertible body style.

The 1963 Corvette Sting Ray had hidden headlights. They flipped up when they were turned on. They flipped back down when they were turned off. It was the first North American car with hidden headlights since the 1942 DeSoto.

The Sting Ray's rear window was split down the middle by a piece called a backbone. The

The 1963 Sting Ray had hidden headlights.

1963 Sting Ray is the only Corvette with the backbone. The backbone makes it valuable to collectors.

Several Firsts

The 1963 Corvette Sting Ray was the first car with a **vertical** radio. The radio dial was changed to fit the vertical format. Every other car radio at the time was **horizontal**.

Buyers of the 1963 model could get several options for the first time ever on a Corvette. The list of options included a leather interior, power steering, power brakes, an AM/FM radio, and air conditioning.

The Sting Ray had no trunk lid. Chevy decided it was too expensive to design one that worked well. Anything the driver carried had to be stuffed behind the seats.

The Sting Ray sold well. Chevy hired a second shift of workers to keep up with the demand for its cars.

The 1964 Sting Ray is as well made as the 1963 model. But it does not have a backbone.

The backbone makes the 1963 Corvette valuable.

Second-generation Corvettes like this 1966 convertible came with four-wheel disc brakes.

That makes the 1964 model less valuable to collectors.

The L-88

In 1965, Chevy put four-wheel **disc brakes** on every new Corvette. Chevy gave the Corvette optional 427-cubic-inch (7,003-cubic-centimeter) V-8 engines.

Other engines included a standard 427-cubic-inch engine that produced 435 horsepower. *Car and Driver* magazine tested a

Corvette with that engine. It accelerated from zero to 60 miles (96 kilometers) per hour in 4.7 seconds.

The other new engine was called the L-88. L-88s were made for racing. They did well at the Daytona Speedway. Cars with L-88s ran laps 10 seconds faster than any of the other cars. But only 216 L-88s were sold to customers from 1967 to 1969. The L-88 was designed for the racetrack, not for the street.

Corvettes with the L-88 engine are valuable to collectors. Only 20 L-88s were sold in 1967. Only three of them are known to exist today. They are some of the most prized Corvettes ever.

Second-generation Corvettes are popular with collectors.

The second generation ended with the 1967 Corvette. Second-generation Corvettes have the best value in the collectible market. They increase in value about 20 percent every year.

The 1970s

A 454-cubic-inch (7,446-cubic-centimeter) engine replaced the 427-cubic-inch (7,003-cubic-centimeter) engine in 1970. It produced 390 horsepower.

In the early 1970s, many people became concerned about the supply of fuel. The Organization of Petroleum Exporting Countries (OPEC) raised the cost of oil. The price of gas went up. This created an **energy crisis**.

As gas prices went up, people wanted their cars to go as many miles as possible on a tank of gas. Fewer buyers wanted their cars to be big and fast. Corvette sales dropped.

The U.S. government set strict new rules for the auto industry. Chevy had to reduce its engine sizes. The Corvette's performance suffered greatly.

Corvettes made in the 1970s did not perform as well as earlier Corvettes.

Throughout most of the 1970s, the Corvette used the standard 350-cubic-inch (5,740-cubic-centimeter) V-8. Corvette engineers worked hard to get the most power and economy out of that engine.

Throughout most of the 1970s, Corvettes used the standard 350-cubic-inch (5,740-cubic-centimeter) V-8.

Milestones

The Corvette reached a **milestone** on March 14, 1977. That was when the 500,000th Corvette drove off the St. Louis assembly line.

Chevy reached another milestone in 1978. That was when the Corvette observed its 25th anniversary. The Indianapolis 500 honored the Corvette by choosing it as the **pace car**. Chevy built a limited-edition Corvette pace car.

The silver and black Corvette pace car was built as a limited edition.

Chapter 4

Modern Corvettes

The Corvette had a bad reputation from 1973 to 1982. Drivers complained of poor performance. They heard squeaks from body panels that did not fit together well.

Because of the complaints, Chevy redesigned the Corvette in 1983. The new model did not come out until 1984. There never was a 1983 Corvette.

The 1984 Corvette was lighter, roomier, and quicker than earlier models. It went from zero to 60 miles (96 kilometers) per hour in 6.4 seconds. Handling was also improved on the 1984 model.

After the complaints of the 1970s and early 1980s, Chevrolet redesigned the Corvette.

The 1986 convertible was offered with anti-lock brakes.

In 1986, Chevy added anti-lock brakes to the Corvette. Anti-lock brakes are controlled by a computer. Anti-lock brakes never lock up the wheels. Cars with anti-lock brakes never skid out of control.

Chevy also added a new anti-theft system in 1986. It is called VATS, which stands for Vehicle Anti-Theft System.

In 1989, the Corvette became the first North American production car with a six-speed manual transmission.

Racing in the 1980s

Corvettes won every race they entered in the 1985, 1986, and 1987 seasons. Other cars such as the Porsche 944 Turbo could stay with the Corvettes for a while, but not for the whole race. Because the competition could not keep up, Corvettes raced in their own challenge series in 1988 and 1989.

The Callaway Twin Turbo

Reeves Callaway is a famous car designer. He is known for **turbocharging** engines. He

The redesigned Corvette was in a class of its own.

has worked with many carmakers, including Alfa-Romeo, BMW, and Volkswagen. He is best known for his work with Corvettes, though.

Callaway developed his first **twin turbo** Corvette in 1986. His turbo engine raised the Corvette's top speed. Callaway's 1986 Corvette reached speeds of 150 miles (240 kilometers) per hour to 180 miles (288 kilometers) per hour.

Chevy built 185 Callaway twin turbos in 1987. These were production models for sale to the public. These cars all sold within six weeks of being announced. Chevy made more of the Callaways in 1988.

The LT-5

The Corvette ZR1 was introduced in 1990. It was nicknamed the King of the Hill. Chevy put a V-8 engine in the ZR1. The engine was called the LT-5. It produced 375 horsepower. It was a racing engine.

Chevy developed the engine with Lotus. Lotus is a carmaker from England. It is known

The ZR1 is often called the King of the Hill.

for making good aluminum engines. Aluminum
is a lightweight metal. Cars with lighter
engines can go faster.

The Lotus-designed engine was made by
Mercury Marine in Stillwater, Oklahoma.
Mercury Marine is not even a car company.

Mercury Marine is known for making excellent aluminum boat engines. They make their engines by hand.

Corvette engineers managed to squeeze 405 horsepower out of the LT-5 in 1993. The 1994-95 Corvette with the LT-5 went from zero to 60 miles (96 kilometers) per hour in 4.9 seconds. It could spin the tires at 70 miles (112 kilometers) per hour.

An Instant Collectible

The ZR1 looks a lot like a regular Corvette, except the rear tires and rear body are wider.

The ZR1 has another special feature called a valet key. The valet key lets the owner limit the engine's output to 200 horsepower. ZR1 owners may want to limit the horsepower when they let other people drive their Corvettes. Otherwise, drivers who are not used to the LT-5's power might accidentally crash and hurt themselves.

The ZR1 looks a lot like a regular Corvette, except for its wider rear tires and rear body.

Corvette quit making the LT-5 at the end of 1995. General Motors has not been racing as much as it used to, either. Corvette racing is now done by private teams. The Corvette is still a successful racer, though.

The LT-5 engine will probably never be made again. There were about 7,000 ZR1s sold. Many people think they will become top collectibles.

New Corvettes

A new generation of Corvettes began with the 1997 model. The new Corvette is powered by a smaller V-8. The engine block is made of cast aluminum to keep it lightweight.

In new Corvettes, the speedometer goes up to 200 miles (320 kilometers) per hour. A black-light system makes the gauges glow at night.

The new Corvette is six inches (15 centimeters) longer than the 1996 model. It is broader and has wider tires.

The new Corvette is also easier to get into, because the door sills are lower. The car is roomy inside. It has a good-sized trunk.

The new Corvettes come in three body styles. One style has a removable roof panel. Another style is a convertible. The third style has a fixed roof.

Prototypes of the new Corvette were seen at car shows before the car became a production model.

Chapter 5
Safety Features

The Corvette was the first production car with a fiberglass body. One of Chevy's drivers rolled a Corvette during a 1953 test drive. The fiberglass body was not damaged. The driver was not injured. Fiberglass proved to be a safe material.

Seat belts became standard equipment in 1956. Safer disc brakes replaced **drum brakes** in 1965. The 1969 Corvette had an ignition lock on the steering column. The steering column connects the steering wheel to the parts that turn the front wheels. The column lock made the car difficult to steal.

The 1965 Corvette had seat belts and disc brakes.

The 1972 Corvette had an alarm system. Stronger bumpers were introduced in 1973. So were steel beams inside the doors. The steel beams protected the driver and any passengers during side collisions.

Shoulder belts became standard equipment in 1974. In 1979, bright halogen headlights replaced standard headlights. Halogen lights use special chemicals to make them brighter.

Safety in the 1990s

An air bag was added to the Corvette's driver's side in 1990. The air bag expands from the steering wheel when an accident occurs. The air bag keeps the driver from being thrown into the steering wheel or going through the windshield.

Extended-mobility tires are another safety feature of the Corvette. These tires are called EMTs. They are also called run-flat tires. EMTs can go up to 200 miles (320 kilometers) without air inside them.

The 1995 Corvette has a shift lock. The shift lock prevents the automatic transmission from

The 1974 Corvette was the first one with shoulder belts.

being shifted out of park unless the brake is applied. The car cannot roll away if it is accidentally shifted out of park.

Corvette engineers keep looking for ways to make the Corvette one of the safest sports cars. They continue to fine-tune its design. The Corvette will continue to capture the hearts of sports car lovers around the world.

The 1958 Corvette Convertible

Glossary

carburetor—the part of an engine that mixes air with fuel spray, using vacuum pressure to pull the mixture into the cylinders

collectibles—cars that car lovers want to own the most. Collectibles are usually rare, or they have special features.

cylinder—can-shaped area of an engine that contains the piston; where fuel is ignited

disc brakes—an efficient type of brake that works by causing two pads to press on either side of a disc that rotates with the wheel

drum brakes—a type of brake that works by causing two pads to press against only one side of a drum that rotates with the wheel. Drum brakes are less efficient than disc brakes.

energy crisis—a scare during the 1970s when the shortage of natural resources was widely realized

fastback—a type of car body that slopes from the roof to the rear bumper

fiberglass—plasticlike material made from glass fibers

fuel-injected—equipped with a system that uses an electric pump to force a fuel and air mixture into the cylinders. Fuel-injection systems are more efficient than carburetion systems.

horizontal—a side-to-side orientation, rather than an up-and-down one

horsepower—a unit used to measure the power of engines and motors

milestone—an important event in a person, place, or thing's history

pace car—a special car that controls the speed of an automobile race when necessary

stick shift—a metal rod with a handle connected to the gears, which must be shifted manually

turbocharging—a system that uses exhaust pressure to force fuel into the cylinders to create more horsepower

twin turbo—a system that uses two turbochargers to increase an engine's horsepower

V-8—an engine with 8 cylinders set in pairs at angles that form the shape of the letter V

vertical—an up-and-down orientation, rather than a side-to-side one

To Learn More

Jay, Jackson. *Super Sports Cars*. Mankato, Minn.: Capstone Press, 1996.

Ready, Kirk L. *Custom Cars*. Minneapolis: Lerner, 1982.

Stephenson, Sallie. *Sports Cars*. Mankato, Minn.: Capstone Press, 1991.

Sutton, Richard. *Car*. New York: Knopf, 1990.

Useful Addresses

Canadian Automobile Sports Clubs
693 Petrolia Road
Downsview, ON M3J 2N6
Canada

Corvettes of Fresno
646 East Sussex Way
Fresno, CA 93704

Florida Corvette Association
744 Lighthouse Drive
North Palm Beach, FL 33408

National Council of Corvette Clubs
3701 South 92nd Street
Milwaukee, WI 53228-1611

Internet Sites

Chip's Hot Corvette Sites
http://members.aol.com:/chippa777/chip1.htm

Chronological History of Corvettes
http://www.islandnet.com/~kpolsson/
vettehis.htm

National Corvette Museum
http://www.ky.net/corvette

Route 66 Corvette Page
http://www.geocities.com/colosseum/1299

Index